This Book Belongs To:

....

....

FIVE-MINUTE TALES *for* THREE Year Olds

FIVE-MINUTE TALES *for* THREE Year Olds

A beautiful collection of original stories

p

Illustrated by Alison Atkins
(John Martin & Artists)

Language consultant: Betty Root

This is a Parragon book
This edition published in 2006

Parragon
Queen Street House
4 Queen Street
Bath BA1 1HE, UK

ISBN 1-40546-954-4

Printed in China

Contents

Teddy Goes Flying

Ronne Randall

Every day, Teddy played in the garden with Jamie. And every day, he looked up at the garden fence – and wondered what was beyond it.

Sometimes Jamie went inside and left Teddy out on his own. Then Teddy would talk to the birds, who came and sat on the fence.

"What's out there?" Teddy asked them.

"You'll have to come and see for yourself," they chirped. "Come and fly with us."

"But I can't fly," Teddy told them. "I'm a bear, not a bird like you."

"Well, then you'll have to find out some other way," said the birds, flying off.

One morning, when they were playing pirates, Jamie accidentally dropped Teddy in a puddle. He went rushing indoors.

"Mum, look at Teddy!" he cried. "He's all wet and muddy!"

"Never mind," said Mum. "I'll just pop him into the washing machine with the towels. He'll soon be nice and clean again!" Into the machine went Teddy.

Swish – swish – swish he went, round and round, while the soap bubbles washed out all the mud. By the time Jamie had finished his lunch, Teddy was nice and clean. But he was still very wet.

"We'll hang him out with the rest of the washing," said Mum. "The fresh air and sunshine will make him dry and fluffy again."

"I'll hang Teddy up by his ears," Jamie said, hurrying to help his mum.

"It's a lovely, breezy afternoon," said Mum. "Teddy's sure to be dry by the time we get back from the shops."

While Jamie and his mum went shopping, Teddy was blowing gently in the breeze. But soon the breeze got stronger … and stronger … until it was a very blustery wind!

Whoosh! Swoosh! went the wind. To and fro went Teddy. Up and down, high and low, until …

Pop! went one peg, and Teddy's ear came loose.

Pop! went the other peg, and Teddy's other ear came loose.

Then Teddy was flying – up over the apple tree and into the air!

"Whee!" Teddy called to the birds. "I'm flying, just like you!"

Up over gardens and rooftops Teddy swept and swooped. He could see everything!

"Now I know what's out in the world!" he thought to himself. "There are trees and houses and gardens full of grass and flowers, just like ours! There are roads and cars, and people walking and riding bikes! There are cats and dogs. There is so much to see!"

Teddy swooped down over one garden where there were swings and a slide and a big climbing-frame.

"What fun Jamie and I could have playing there!" he thought.

A moment later he was swept up again, and he zoomed over another garden. He watched a dog burying his bone in a flower-bed.

"Look at me!" Teddy called to the dog. "I'm flying!"

"Woof!" called the surprised dog. "I've never seen a teddy-bird before!"

High and low went Teddy, looking at everything as he soared and glided and dipped and flipped. He had never, ever had so much fun!

But after a while, Teddy had had enough flying for one day. He was getting tired of whirling and twirling, and swooping and soaring. He had seen all he wanted to see. Teddy was ready to be back down on the ground, where he could feel something besides air underneath him.

"How do I stop flying?" he asked the birds.

"Easy!" they told him. "Just stop flapping your wings!"

"But I haven't got any wings!" said Teddy.

"Then you shouldn't be flying!" said the birds.

"You're right," moaned Teddy. "I'm not a bird, I'm a bear – and I don't belong up in the air! It's much too breezy, and my tummy's all queasy! What can I do?" But the birds just flapped their wings and flew off into the trees.

Luckily, the wind was starting to slow down a bit, so Teddy began slowing down, too. Then …

"Oh! Oh! Oh! Help! I'm falling!"

From the treetops, the birds watched – but they couldn't do anything to help Teddy!

Teddy fell down, down, all the way down to the ground, and … Splash! into another big puddle, right in front of Jamie's house.

At that moment, Jamie and his mum were coming home from their shopping trip.

"Mum, look!" cried Jamie, running ahead. "It's Teddy! What's he doing out here?"

"The wind must have blown him off the line," said Mum.

Jamie bent down to pick up his bear. "He's all right," he said, "but he's very wet and muddy again!"

"Then we'll have to pop him back into the washing machine," said Mum. "Only this time," she added, as she felt the breeze pick up, "I think we'll let him dry in the airing cupboard!"

"Good idea," said Jamie.

"A very good idea!" thought Teddy.

Ben's Boots

Jillian Harker

Ben really loved his shiny blue boots, so he wore them whenever he could. If Ben looked out of the window in the morning and saw that it was raining, a big smile would spread across his face. He would run downstairs and pull on his blue boots straight away, ready to splash in the puddles on his way to Nursery.

When the rain stopped, Ben would keep his boots on, so that he could squelch around in the patches of squidgy mud that the rain left.

Even when it was hot, Ben would wear his boots to slosh round and round in the paddling pool. He thought he could make much bigger splashes with his boots on than in bare feet. Ben's blue boots were great fun!

One morning Ben peeped out of his window, to check if it was raining. When he saw that it was, he hurried downstairs and started to pull his boots on. But it wasn't quite as easy as usual.

He was busy tugging at them when Mum suddenly said, "Those boots look tight. I think you've grown too big for them. We'll have to get you some new ones."

"I don't want new ones," said Ben at once. "I like my boots. I want to keep them."

"You can't wear boots that are too small, Ben," said Mum. "They'll hurt your feet. We'll go to the shoe shop after Nursery."

So that's what they did.

The lady in the shoe shop brought red boots, yellow boots and green boots for Ben to try.

"I'm very sorry," she explained to Ben's mum, "we don't have any blue boots left in your little boy's size."

"I don't want any new blue boots," muttered Ben. "I want my old ones." But Mum was very firm.

"You'll have to try these on, Ben," she said. "Your old boots are too small."

In the end, Mum bought Ben a pair of bright yellow boots.

"They look really good, Ben," Mum told him.

"No they don't!" thought Ben. "And I'm not going to wear them!"

As soon as they got home, Ben ran to the cupboard under the stairs and got out his old blue boots. He tugged and pulled until he got them on. Then he went into the kitchen for tea. Mum saw the boots, and smiled.

"Okay," she said. "You can wear your blue boots for one last time. But once they come off, that's it. Next time you must wear the yellow ones." Ben thought hard. He knew what to do – he wouldn't take his blue boots off at all. Then he wouldn't have to wear the yellow ones.

All through tea, Ben kept saying, "I like my blue boots. They're not too small, they're just right."

"Story time," said Mum, after tea. "Come and take your boots off and sit here with me." Usually Ben loved to snuggle up to Mum on the sofa when she read him a story, but there was no way he was going to take his boots off. He sat stiff and straight next to Mum as she read him his favourite book.

"Right, Ben," Mum said, as she closed the book. "Let's get those boots off. It's time for bed, and you can't wear boots in bed."

"Yes I can," said Ben, running up the stairs and jumping into bed. "I can sleep in boots, can't I, Ted?" Ben grabbed his favourite teddy and held him tight.

Mum came into the bedroom. She was wondering how she was going to get Ben to take off his boots. He loved them more than anything, except his teddy, she thought. And that was when Mum had an idea.

"Poor Ted," she said. "What's he going to do now?"

"What do you mean?" asked Ben.

"I thought he could have your blue boots, Ben," said Mum, "so he could come out with you to play when it's wet. But if you won't take them off ..."

"Oh!" said Ben. This was really difficult. Ben loved his blue boots, but he loved his teddy too.

He couldn't keep his old boots if Ted needed them, could he? And it would be great to take Ted out in the rain with him. Ben thought hard. He looked at the new yellow boots standing by his wardrobe. They did look like they could be fun too.

He would do it! He would take off the blue boots and wear the yellow boots, after all.

Ben tugged off his blue boots. He slipped them onto Ted's feet.

"They really suit Ted!" said Mum, smiling.

"Can he keep them on?" asked Ben.

"Of course he can," smiled Mum.

"Well, if Ted's going to wear his boots in bed, can I wear mine too?" asked Ben.

"Okay," laughed Mum. "Just this once!" She handed the yellow boots to Ben. He slipped them on and lifted his feet up to show Ted.

"Ben's boots!" he said proudly.

Poor Humphrey

Jan Payne

Humphrey was a baby rhino and he wasn't at all happy. Once he used to whistle all day long, but he could no longer do that. Now he sat with his back to the other animals, wearing a cardboard box on his head!

One day, Rory the lion cub called to see if Humphrey could come out to play.

"Humpy!" called Mum. "Rory's here. He wants you to play snakes and ladders. He's brought the snakes with him!"

"Don't want to," answered Humphrey in a cross voice.

"Come on, Humpy!" said Mum, encouragingly.

"Don't call me Humpy," came the reply.

Then Maureen the elephant called to see if Humpy could go swimming.

"Shan't!" came the response,

"and my name's NOT Humpy!"

Shall I tell you why Humphrey was so sad? He had a "nobbly thing" on his face instead of a spike, and he didn't like it one little bit. Mum said it would grow into a spike one day, but "one day" seemed a very long way off. So Humphrey refused to go out unless he was wearing his cardboard box. That way the "nobbly thing" would be hidden, and no one would laugh at him – absolutely no one.

Mum got cross because Humphrey wore the cardboard box all the time.

"You can't eat with that thing on your head," she would say when she saw Humphrey trying to poke food through one of the holes.

"How can I wash behind your ears, you silly thing?" she would laugh when she tried to give him a bath. And if he got a cold and tried to blow his nose, well – you've never seen such a mess!

One lovely sunny day, Humphrey was really fed up staying indoors. He just had to go outside.

"Be careful!" said Mum, as he set off.

Humphrey stumbled along trying to look at things through the holes in his box. He saw a lizard on a rock, staring at him. He sniffed a red flower growing on a bush. He watched an army of ants carrying things on their backs.

Humphrey hadn't gone very far when a deep voice said, "Watch where you're going, Humpy!"

Humphrey noticed it had got quite dark. He recognized Big Elephant's voice but couldn't see where the voice was coming from.

"Where are you?" asked Humphrey.

"Right above you," said Big Elephant.

Humphrey had walked right under Big Elephant. "Sorry," he said, " I didn't see you. And my name's not Humpy!" he added as he moved away.

Humphrey had not gone much farther when he heard giggling. He felt a tug at his box.

"Oi!" he shouted.

"Oi, yourself!" said a voice, and the box was whisked off Humphrey's head. It was Monkey. He grinned down at Humphrey, holding the box in his hands.

"Now what?" he giggled.

"Bring it back or I'll ..." shouted Humphrey.

"Or I'll, or I'll ..." taunted Monkey.

But Monkey wasn't really a bad monkey – he was just naughty. He was sorry when he saw Humphrey was getting upset.

"Here you are, Humpy," he said, giving Humphrey the box.

Humphrey was cross. He put the box back on his head. "You're a pest," he said, "and don't call me Humpy!"

By now Humphrey's walk was ruined. He sat for a while under a tree feeling very sorry for himself. Then he heard the sound of singing and laughing. The sound instantly cheered him up.

Into the clearing came a group of baby rhinos. And guess what! They were all wearing cardboard boxes on their heads, just like Humphrey. They stopped when they saw him.

"What's your name?" asked one little rhino.

"Humpy," said Humphrey, without thinking.

"That's a nice name," said another rhino. "I'm Dora. Won't you come and play with us, Humpy?" she asked.

It was funny, but Humphrey didn't seem to mind when Dora called him Humpy. He stayed in the clearing all afternoon, playing games, singing songs and telling rhino jokes. The baby rhinos all agreed to meet there every Tuesday and Thursday.

Humphrey was so happy he would have skipped home if rhinos could skip! He thought Dora would probably be his very best friend ever.

One day not long after, Humphrey put on his best box to go out. When he did this, it ripped right down the front. Grumbling, he got out his second-best box, and put that on. His second-best box ripped as well.

"Stupid boxes!" said Humphrey. He felt the front of his face. There was something there. Something sharp.

He went to the water's edge and looked at his reflection. Woah! There it was, plain as the nose on your face. The "nobbly thing" had gone and Humphrey had a beautiful pointy spike.

"Mum," yelled Humphrey, "come and see!"

"I told you so," said Mum, hugging him.

"From now on, my name is Spike," said Humphrey proudly. And off he went, without his box, to meet his new friends.

And do you know what? They weren't wearing boxes any more, either!

The Remembering Fairy

Clive Batkin

Georgina's mum was terribly forgetful. Georgina never noticed this when she was very little. Now that she was old enough to go to nursery it was a nuisance!

Every day, Mum would forget something important. One morning she would forget to have Georgina's bag ready, the next she would forget to make her any lunch. When Georgina needed her PE kit, Mum would forget to wash it. When it was time to go to nursery, Mum would forget where she had put her car keys. Sometimes, Mum even forgot it was a nursery day at all, and let Georgina sleep very late!

Georgina tried to help her mum remember things. She would leave little notes for her on the fridge door or on the hall table, but Mum would always walk past and forget to look at them.

Georgina had a very kind teacher called Mrs Jones, who tried to help by meeting Mum at the school gate and giving her special reminders. She'd say things like, "Don't forget about the nature walk tomorrow – Georgie will need her wellies!" Or "Don't forget to come along for parents' day tomorrow!" But, of course, by the next day Mum would have completely forgotten that she'd spoken to Mrs Jones!

One particular day, Georgina was feeling very miserable. Mum had forgotten that today was Fancy-Dress Day, and had not made Georgina a costume.

The other children came to nursery dressed as clowns and ballerinas, or as wild animals and monsters. Georgina was just wearing her normal clothes! Georgina sat all alone in the playground as the other children played pretending games.

"I wish there was a way I could make Mum remember things," she said sadly.

Suddenly, there was a puff of smoke and sparkle at Georgina's shoulder.

"I can help!" said a little voice. Georgina jumped up.

"What was that?" she wondered out loud.

"It was me!" said the little voice. "I can help your mum remember things."

"But who are you?" said Georgina. "And where are you?"

She couldn't see anyone!

"Ah, I'm very hard to find!" laughed the voice. "But I'm right here beside you!"

Georgina looked all around her. Finally she saw a tiny fairy hovering near her ear.

"I'm the Remembering Fairy," said the fairy, "and I'm here to help."

"But how can you help?" asked Georgina, feeling very confused.

"I help people like your mum remember things," said the fairy. "Whenever they are about to forget something important, I pop up and whisper in their ear."

Georgina looked doubtful.

"Cheer up!" said the fairy. "You're not the first little girl or boy to have forgetful parents, you know."

"Really?"

"Of course not," said the fairy. "Why, just this morning I had to help a little boy's dad remember how to tie his shoe laces."

"Wow! Maybe that's why Mum asked Mrs Jones to teach me to tie my laces," laughed Georgina.

"Oh yes, you'd be amazed what people forget," laughed the fairy. "So, don't you worry about a thing! Next time your mum is about to forget something, I'll be there!"

"Thank you," said Georgina.

The fairy smiled, and disappeared in another puff of smoke and sparkle.

"Well," thought Georgina, "what a helpful fairy."

At the end of nursery that day, there was no sign of Georgina's mum. "Don't worry, Georgina," said Mrs Jones, "I'm sure she'll be here soon." Just then, Mum came running down the road.

"I'm sorry I'm late," she puffed. "I was shopping and completely forgot the time."

Georgina had heard this excuse before.

"But then an amazing thing happened," said Mum. "I was thinking about what I needed to buy for tea, when I heard a little voice in my ear whispering, 'Don't forget to pick Georgina up from nursery.' It really was the strangest thing."

Georgina smiled to herself.

Next morning, Georgina came down to breakfast. She was surprised to see Mum waiting for her with her bag already packed.

"I've got everything ready for you, Georgie," said Mum. "Your lunch, your crayons, your sports clothes – everything you need for nursery today."

"Jolly good, Mum," said Georgina happily.

"Well, I think I heard that voice again, telling me what to get ready," said Mum. "It really is very strange indeed ..."

The next few days were the same. Every time Mum had something important to remember, the Remembering Fairy popped up and whispered in her ear.

After two weeks with the Remembering Fairy, Georgina's mum found she was starting to remember things more and more. And she was beginning to hear the strange little voice in her ear less and less.

"You know," said Mum, "I really think my memory is getting much better."

Georgina heard a familiar puff of smoke and sparkle near her ear.

"Well, Georgina," whispered the fairy, "I think my job here is done."

Georgina smiled. "Mum does seem really good at remembering things now. Thank you so much, fairy."

"I'm pleased to help," said the fairy, and in a flash she was gone.

Georgina hasn't seen the fairy again since, but she always keeps an eye out for that special puff of smoke and sparkle – she certainly won't forget the Remembering Fairy!

Jack and the Mice

Ronne Randall

Katy Cat strolled out of the house into the garden. "It's a beautiful, warm, sunny day," she thought. "A perfect day to give Jack his first mouse-catching lesson."

Jack was Katy Cat's kitten. He had only been out in the garden a few times, and had never seen a mouse. But Katy Cat knew that would change soon. She went back into the house to get Jack.

At the other end of the garden, Mitzi Mouse came out of her nest and looked around.

"It's a beautiful, warm, sunny day," she said to herself. "And it looks as if the coast is clear. It's a perfect day to give Miles and Melanie their first lesson in finding food in the garden – and keeping away from cats!"

Miles and Melanie were Mitzi's children, and they had never seen a cat. But Mitzi knew that would change soon.

Back near the house, Jack trotted out into the sunshine beside his mum.

"I'm going to teach you about mice," Katy Cat said to Jack. "It's our job to catch mice, you know."

Jack liked catching things. He was especially good at catching dust balls and fluff, so this sounded like fun.

"What do mice look like?" he asked his mum. "Do they look like dust balls?"

"A little," she replied. "But they are much more annoying. They might be brown or grey, and they have long tails and wiggly whiskers. They move very fast," said Katy Cat, "but you must move faster – and catch them!"

Jack nodded. "I will, Mum," he promised.

At the other end of the garden, Mitzi Mouse had brought Miles and Melanie out of the nest.

"The best places to look for food," she told them, "are by the raspberry canes and in the vegetable patch. But you must watch out for cats!"

"What's a cat?" asked Miles and Melanie together.

"Cats are very dangerous creatures," their mother explained. "They are big and furry, and they have sharp teeth and claws, and twitchy whiskers. They move very fast," she told them, "but you must move faster – and run away from them!"

Miles and Melanie both nodded. "We will, Mum," they promised.

A little while later, as his mum stretched out to sleep in the sun, Jack padded out into the grass. Feeling very brave and important, he sniffed all around and twitched his whiskers as he looked around for mice.

Not far away, while their mum had a rest in their nest, Miles and Melanie went out to scout for food. With their whiskers wiggling and their tails twittering, they scurried to the raspberry canes.

Jack saw the two little creatures running through the grass.

"Stop!" he called.

Miles and Melanie froze and stared at him.

"Are you mice?" Jack asked them.

"Y-yes," said Miles.

"Are you a cat?" asked Melanie.

"Yes," said Jack. He looked at them. "I think I'm supposed to catch you."

"And I'm sure we're supposed to run away from you!" said Miles.

"Our mum said you were dangerous!" said Melanie.

"And my mum said you were annoying," said Jack. "But you look friendly to me."

"So do you," said Miles.

"I'd rather play than catch you!" said Jack.

"And we'd rather play than run away!" said Melanie.

"Maybe I can be dangerous and catch you tomorrow," said Jack.

"Okay!" said Miles and Melanie.

So Jack and Miles and Melanie began to play together. First, they played hide-and-seek – Jack hid behind the apple tree, and Miles and Melanie hid in the vegetable patch. Of course, they all found each other in the end.

Then, they played roll-the-raspberry – Jack managed to catch every raspberry that Miles and Melanie rolled! Then, they played shadow-jumping and leapmouse.

The three friends were right in the middle of a wonderful game of tag when Katy Cat looked up and saw Jack chasing Miles and Melanie.

"That's right, Jack," she called. "Get them!"

Jack looked back at his mum. "Run!" he whispered to the mice.

At that moment, Mitzi Mouse came out of her nest and saw her children running away from Jack.

"That's right!" she called to them. "Run, run, as fast as you can!"

As Miles and Melanie ran away, Jack padded back to his mum.

"Never mind," said Katy, licking his ear. "That was very good for your first time. You'll do better tomorrow."

And on the other side of the garden, Mitzi Mouse told her children, "I'm so glad you're safe! We have plenty of food for now. You can look for more tomorrow."

Just before they went inside, Miles and Melanie looked back at Jack. And Jack looked back at them.

All three winked, then gave a little wave with their tails and twitched their whiskers. It was their way of letting each other know they'd be back again tomorrow – to have lots more fun together!

The Selfish Puppy

Gaby Goldsack

Everyone adored Bonnie. She was the biggest, prettiest, cleverest puppy in the litter. Wherever she went everyone fussed over her.

"Oh, what silky fur you have," said her mother, licking her fur gently.

"You're so big and strong," laughed her father as he watched her play with her smaller brothers.

"What a clever little girl," said her owner, when Bonnie was the first of the puppies to walk. There was no doubt about it, Bonnie was the best puppy around. And, of course, Bonnie loved all the praise.

"I suppose I am rather special," she said, as she gazed at her reflection in the mirror.

Oh, yes, EVERYONE adored Bonnie. Well, not quite everyone. The other three puppies were not always so keen on their sister. You see, as well as being the biggest, prettiest, smartest puppy in the litter, Bonnie was also the most selfish.

But Bonnie didn't know that she was selfish. She didn't even know what the word selfish meant. Because she was always being told how special she was, she just thought that she, and only she, deserved nothing but the very best. So when it came to mealtimes, she always made sure that she got the largest, juiciest share.

"Out the way," she'd bark, as she pushed past the smaller puppies. "I've got to keep my strength up."

When it came to bedtime, she always made sure that she got the comfiest spot beside the fire. "I've got to keep warm," she'd explain, as she shoved whoever was there out of the way.

And, worst of all, she would never let the other puppies play with the toys. "You'll only spoil them," she'd say. "You're just not as careful as me."

Her behaviour made the other puppies cross. One day, after Bonnie had eaten all the food without offering them so much as a nibble, they were crosser than ever.

"Just who does she think she is?" snapped Ben, the biggest boy puppy.

"She thinks she's special," said Bill, the next brother.

"She is special," squeaked Titch, the smallest pup of them all. "After all, everyone is always saying she is."

"She may be special," grunted Ben, "but I've had enough.

From now on, I'm going to stay out of her way."

"Me too," agreed Bill.

"And me," squeaked Titch.

And from then on, the three little pups did just that. Bonnie didn't notice at first, she was far too busy being selfish. But after a while, she started to feel lonely, so she went to find her brothers. They were playing with a ball.

"Play with me," she demanded. And she snatched the ball right out of Titch's mouth.

Ben, Bill and Titch were furious.

"I think I'll go and play somewhere else," barked Ben.

"Me too," growled Bill.

"And me," squeaked Titch.

"Wait for me," called Bonnie. But the puppies had already disappeared.

A few minutes later, she found them cuddling up next to their mother and father.

"Mum, Dad," whined Bonnie. "They won't play with me. It's just not fair. After all, I am a very SPECIAL puppy."

"Oh, dear," said her mother. "I think it's about time we had a little chat."

Bonnie cocked her head and pulled her cutest face. Surely Mum was about to tell her she was right.

"You are very special," began her mother.

"Told you so," sang Bonnie, smiling at her brothers.

"But so are Bill, Ben and Titch," said her mother.

Bonnie looked shocked. Surely she was extra special, wasn't she?

"But they won't play with me," she whined.

"Well," said her mother. "Have you been playing nicely with them? Have you been sharing things?"

"Well ... no," whispered Bonnie.

Her mother shook her head sadly. "Perhaps you should try sharing things, then you might find that your brothers will want to play with you."

"Really," whispered Bonnie, looking doubtfully at the other puppies.

Bill, Ben and Titch wagged their tails.

"And you never know," added her father. "You might even discover that sharing things is fun!"

Bonnie wasn't at all sure about this sharing thing. But that afternoon she decided to let the other puppies have a turn at snoozing in front of the fire. The next morning, she made sure that each of them had an equal share of food. And in the afternoon she showed them her secret store of bones.

Bill, Ben and Titch were delighted.

"Thanks," squeaked Titch, giving her a big lick.

"Let's play hide-and-seek," cried Bill.

And the four puppies spent the rest of the day playing together happily.

Later that night, all four of them curled up together in front of the fire.

"You were right" smiled Bonnie, turning to her parents. "Sharing really is fun."

"What's that?" asked Mum. She was too busy nudging Dad to take any real notice.

"Look, can't you just budge over," said Dad, as he attempted to push Mum out of the way. "You're taking all the room."

"Excuse me!" coughed Bonnie. "Remember 'sharing things is fun'."

"Oh, yes," laughed Mum and Dad. They gave each other more space. "Sharing really is fun."

And Bill, Ben and Titch wagged their tails in agreement.

Backstroke Benny

Ronne Randall

Mama Duck looked at her four new ducklings. There were two boy ducklings and two girl ducklings, and each one was fluffy and beautiful.

She decided to name the boy ducklings Benny and Kenny. She called the girl ducklings Jenny and Penny.

Mama Duck caught the best flies and slugs and snails she could find and brought them to her babies for dinner.

"You need all this good food, so you can become strong swimmers," she told them.

"When will we start swimming, Mama?" Jenny asked.

"When you can flap your feet properly," she told them.

Every day the ducklings tried flapping their feet in the nest, to see if they were ready to swim.

"I can't wait!" Kenny said. "I think I will be the best swimmer of all."

"No, I will!" said Jenny.

"You will all be fine swimmers," said Mama Duck. "The finest on the lake!"

One bright, sunny day, after the ducklings had been flapping their feet for hours, Mama Duck decided the time had come.

"Get ready for your first swim, my dears!" she told her ducklings. "Line up behind me."

The ducklings did as they were told. Kenny was first, then Jenny, then Penny. Benny was last of all.

Mama Duck marched down to the lake, and all her ducklings followed – one, two, three, four.

Mama Duck slid into the water, and all her ducklings followed – one, two, three, four.

"Now," said Mama Duck, when everyone was in the water, "stay right behind me, flap your feet, and – SWIM!"

Kenny flapped his feet, and swam right behind Mama.

Jenny flapped her feet, and swam right behind Kenny.

Penny flapped her feet, and swam right behind Jenny.

And Benny flapped his feet, and swam ... backwards!

"Wait! Wait for me!" Benny called, flapping his feet as fast as he could.

His brother and sisters all turned around. So did Mama Duck.

"Benny, come back!" called Jenny, Penny and Kenny.

"You're doing the backstroke," called Mama Duck. "You need to flap your feet forward!"

Benny tried to flap his feet forward, but they wouldn't go. He just went backwards faster.

"It's no use!" he called. "I can only swim backwards!"

Benny's family tried to help. They pushed him, they pulled him, they spun him round.

But no matter what they did, Benny could only swim one way – backwards!

Near the shore, two geese watched and laughed.

"Look at him!" they honked. "He can't even swim straight! What kind of duck does he think he is?"

And they laughed and laughed.

Benny hung his head to hide his tears. Jenny, Kenny and Penny tried to cheer him up, but Mama Duck was furious.

"How dare you laugh at my duckling!" she quacked at the geese. "Why does everyone have to swim the same way? I'll bet you can't do the backstroke! You should be ashamed of yourselves, laughing at a youngster!"

The geese knew she was right.

"Sorry, Benny," they said quietly.

That made Benny feel better, and he was ready to start swimming with the others again. Of course, he had to turn around so that he was swimming in the same direction as everyone else.

As they swam along the lake, Jenny, Penny and Kenny told him what they could see up ahead.

"I see two horses galloping in the field," said Kenny.

"I see four cows munching grass," said Jenny.

"I see two rabbits chasing each other round the lake," said Penny.

And Benny told them what he could see happening behind them.

"The horses have stopped galloping, because someone's bringing them some carrots," he told the others.

"Two of the cows are lying down to rest," he said.

"The rabbits have run away, and a fox is coming out of the apple orchard," he said.

"A fox?" said his brother and sisters.

"A FOX?" honked the geese.

"A FOX!" quacked Mama Duck. "Quick! We have to get away!"

"Follow me!" said Benny, swimming to the front of the line. "I can see the fox, so I can lead everyone away from him!"

Doing the backstroke, Benny guided his family away from the fox. The geese came, too. They all followed Benny to the tall marsh grass, where they hid safely until the fox went away.

When the fox was gone, everyone breathed a sigh of relief. Then they gathered round Benny.

"Benny, your backstroke saved the day," said Mama Duck. "I'm so proud of you!"

"You're a hero!" said Penny.

"Can you teach us to do the backstroke?" asked Jenny and Kenny.

"We'll never make fun of your swimming again," the geese promised. "Three cheers for Backstroke Benny!"

As everyone cheered, Mama Duck watched proudly. "I knew all my ducklings would be fine swimmers," she thought, "but even I didn't know just how special Backstroke Benny would be!"

Smile, Please!

Jillian Harker

"What's the matter, Mum?" Danny asked at breakfast one morning. "You look a bit worried."

"I just can't think of anything to get Granny for her birthday present," said Mum.

"What about a nice bunch of flowers?" Dad suggested. "She loves them."

"But we always get her flowers," Mum replied. "I wanted to give her something different. Has anyone got any other good ideas?"

"I have," said Josie before her brother or her dad could answer.

Josie was only three. She was the youngest in the family. "I know what Granny would like," she said. Everyone looked at her.

"What?" they all asked at once.

"A photo of us!" said Josie.

"What a good idea! Granny's always saying she wishes she could see more of us," said Mum. "She really would like a photo of all the family. I'll try to sort out the photographer for Saturday morning." And she did.

Everyone got up very early on Saturday morning. They all put on their best clothes. It wasn't long before Mr Toogood, the photographer, arrived and set up lots of special lights in the sitting room. He asked everyone to take their places.

Mum and Dad sat in the middle of the sofa, and Danny and Josie sat at each end. Josie was next to Dad and Danny was next to Mum.

"Perfect!" said Mr Toogood. "All the family together. Now, I'd like you to smile, please."

Everyone smiled ... except Josie. Mr Toogood looked at her. "Smile, please, Josie," he said.

"But this isn't all the family," said Josie. "Snuffles should be in the picture too." Snuffles was Josie's hamster.

"She is part of the family," agreed Danny.

"It's fine by me," said Mr Toogood.

Mum nodded, and Josie ran off to fetch Snuffles. When she came back with the hamster, Josie was covered in bits of straw. It was stuck all over her best clothes.

"Oh dear," said Mum. "Just look at you." She tried to pull off some of the pieces of straw, but Mr Toogood was in a bit of a hurry to take the photo.

"Everyone ready?" he asked. They all nodded … except Josie.

"I want Wilbur in the photo," she said. Wilbur was the family cat.

"Would you like to fetch him?" sighed Mr Toogood.

Josie handed the hamster to Danny and ran off. Wilbur was asleep on the kitchen windowsill.

It was warm there, and he was having a lovely dream, so he wasn't very happy to be woken up.

"Miaow!" he wailed, as Josie carried him back to the sofa.

"Everyone ready?" asked Mr Toogood. "Smile, please!"

"Just a minute," said Josie.

"What's the matter now?" asked Dad.

"It won't be right without Cuddles," said Josie. Cuddles was Josie's favourite teddy bear.

"Well, he is sort of family," smiled Dad.

"Make it quick!" said Mum. Josie handed the cat to Mum and went off to fetch Cuddles. But she wasn't very quick, because she couldn't remember exactly where she had left her teddy. She couldn't find him anywhere in her room. Mum started to call

her name. Then Josie suddenly thought to look under the bed. And there was Cuddles! She took him downstairs.

"Right. Here we go, at last," said Mum, trying to stay calm.

Josie took her place on the sofa, hugging Cuddles. Wilbur purred on Mum's lap. Snuffles slept in Danny's arms. Everyone began to smile ... except Josie. A big tear began to trickle down her cheek.

"Oh dear," said Mr Toogood. "What's the matter?" asked Dad.

"Granny will be sad if Jumble isn't in the photo. She loves Jumble."

It was true. Granny did love their dog, Jumble. But no one remembered seeing him all morning. Everyone shouted his name. Then they waited. There was a pattering sound in the hall and Jumble dashed into the sitting room. His paws were covered in dirt and his fur was very messy. He had a bone in his mouth.

He leapt up onto Danny. The hamster woke up and scrambled up Danny and onto his head. Jumble jumped onto Mum's lap. The cat woke up and jumped onto Mum's shoulder. Jumble jumped again.

"Woof!" he barked loudly, as he landed on Dad's lap. He wagged his tail in Dad's face.

"Smile, PLEASE!" shouted Mr Toogood. And Josie smiled. Everyone else burst out laughing. Mr Toogood pressed the button on his camera.

"At last!" he said.

"What will Granny think?" asked Mum.

"Granny will love it," said Josie.

And Josie was right. Granny did love the photo. It made her smile too.

The Very Serious Lion Cub

Gaby Goldsack

Bantu was a very serious little lion cub. He never smiled and he never ever laughed. You see, Bantu was the son of Addo, King of the Jungle, and he knew that one day he, too, would become king. And the thought of following in his father's HUGE footsteps worried Bantu. After all, the animals were always saying how great Addo was, how good he was, how kind he was and, above all, how WISE he was. Bantu didn't know how he was ever going to be all those things.

Oh, yes, following in Addo's footsteps definitely worried Bantu.

King Addo tried his best to bring a smile to his son's face. He knew that only a happy lion would make a good king. "Don't worry," he'd laugh. "I'll be around for a long time yet. There's plenty of time for you to learn all about becoming king. And there's no reason why you shouldn't have fun along the way." But Bantu simply stared at him.

As time passed and Bantu got more and more serious, King Addo became more and more unhappy. He couldn't bear to see his only son so sad. And, as King Addo got more and more unhappy, so did all the other animals.

Eventually, an air of gloom descended on the once happy jungle.

Then,
one day,
King Addo
decided that enough
was enough. He called
a jungle meeting.

"Tomorrow we're going to have a contest," he announced. "A contest to make my son, Bantu, laugh. Whoever makes him laugh first, will be made king for a day."

The jungle animals gasped. Then they started to chatter excitedly among themselves. Everyone wanted to take part. Everyone wanted to win. Everyone wanted to be king for a day. But, above all, everyone wanted to see the little lion cub laugh.

The following afternoon, everyone met beside the watering hole. A miserable looking Bantu sat beside his father as the other animals tried to get his attention.

"Us first. Us first," bellowed the hippos, who were all wearing pink tutus.

"Very well," roared the king. "Let the entertainment begin."

As the hefty hippos stumbled and bumbled their way through a hilarious ballet, everyone watched Bantu for the merest hint of a smile. But, even though they bashed and crashed, bounced and flounced, as only hippos performing ballet can, Bantu's lips didn't so much as twitch.

Next to take the stage were the amazing miming chimpanzees, whose speciality was doing imitations of other jungle animals.

"Ah, these guys should make you laugh," King Addo told Bantu. But Bantu remained grim, even when they did a splashy impression of an elephant taking a quiet bath. In fact, only Choto the chimp looked more miserable than Bantu. Choto was sulking because he'd been told that he couldn't take part in the act because he just wasn't funny. "It's not fair," moaned Choto, as he nibbled on a banana. "I'm as funny as the other chimps."

After the chimpanzees came the laughing hyenas, followed by the wrestling rhinos and the gyrating giraffes. But none of the acts brought so much as a smile to Bantu's lips.

As the last giraffe waltzed off the stage, King Addo rose sadly.

"I would like to thank you all," he sighed, as he paced up and down. "But it would appear that nothing can make my little Bantu laugh."

"Ha!" sulked Choto the chimp, as he finished his banana. "I wasn't even given a chance." And, without thinking what he was doing, he tossed his banana skin to the ground.

"Watch out," cried Bantu, as King Addo slipped off the bank. But he was too late.

"Ahhhhhh," roared King Addo, as he skidded on the banana skin and landed headfirst in the watering hole.

"Oh dear," cried Choto, as the mighty lion shook his massive head and squirted water out of his mouth.

"Oooooh," gasped Bantu. Then his lips began to twitch, and his chin began to wobble. Then, much to King Addo's amazement, Bantu began to laugh. The laughing got louder and louder, until, before long, he was rolling about on the ground.

"S...s...sorry, Father," he hiccuped. "But you just look sooooo funny. Perhaps following in your footsteps won't be so difficult, after all."

The other animals held their breath. After all, no one laughed at their mighty king. But then, King Addo's lips twitched and before long he, too, was rolling around with laughter. And, one by one, the other animals joined in.

"Th...thanks," spluttered King Addo, thumping Choto on the back. "I think you'll make a brilliant king for the day."

On hearing this, everyone laughed louder than ever. But no one laughed louder than Bantu the lion cub.

King Addo smiled proudly. He knew that one day his son would make a wonderful king.

Jasmine's Summer Lullaby

Clive Batkin

One warm summer's night, Jasmine just could not get to sleep. The next day was her birthday and she was very excited. She couldn't wait for the morning when she could open all the birthday cards and presents that the postman would bring. She tossed and turned, pulled up the blankets, plumped up her pillow, tried counting sheep – but nothing made her sleepy!

"What I really need is someone to sing me a lullaby," she muttered to herself.

A small bird sitting in the big old oak tree outside Jasmine's bedroom window heard this.

"I'll sing her one of our bird lullabies," it thought. It flew onto Jasmine's windowsill and opened its beak.

"Tweet, tweet, tweet – Jasmine go to sleep!" it sang in a gentle twittering voice.

"What a nice song," thought Jasmine. "I like the sound, but it's not making me sleepy."

Jasmine's goldfish had also heard Jasmine wish for a lullaby.

"I know a song that might work," it thought to itself. It opened its mouth and began to sing a goldfish lullaby.

"Bubble, bubble, bubble – sleep or there'll be trouble!" it sang.

To Jasmine, this song just sounded like lots of bubbly water and splashing.

"What a funny sound," she thought, "and it's just making me even more awake!"

The sound of the bird and the fish had woken the family cat.

"I can sing a much better lullaby than that awful bird or that strange fish!" it thought. The cat got up and padded over to Jasmine's bed.

Sticking its head over the side, the cat started to purr its own lullaby.

"Meow, meow, meow – start sleeping now!" it sang.

Jasmine scratched the cat between its ears.

"Thanks for trying to help, Puss," she said, "but your meowing is a bit too loud. It keeps me awake."

Just then, Jasmine's dog got off its pillow where it always slept.

"Out of my way, Cat," it growled, "I've got just the right doggy lullaby for Jasmine."

He opened his large slobbery mouth and began to sing in a gruff voice.

"Woof, woof, bark – little girls sleep when it's dark!"

Jasmine loved her dog, but its barking was the loudest lullaby yet, and Jasmine was more wide awake than ever.

"Thanks for trying, Dog, but I don't think anything is going to make me feel sleepy tonight," said Jasmine.

Suddenly, Jasmine's bedroom door opened – it was Mum, coming to see what all the noise was about.

"What's going on here – what's all this noise?" she asked. "Jasmine, you should be fast asleep by now!"

"I know, Mummy," sighed Jasmine, "but I just can't sleep."

"Well, how about if I sing you the lullaby my mother used to sing me?" said Mum. "It always used to send me to sleep."

Jasmine snuggled up against her mum to listen.

Mum gently began to sing a soft lullaby. Jasmine didn't recognize the words, but the tune was one of the most lovely and soothing things she had ever heard. After a while, very quietly, all the animals began to join in with her mother's singing. The bird sang along in its twittering voice. The goldfish made its bubbling and plopping sounds, the cat sat next to the bed, purring gently. The dog woofed along in its most quiet and soothing voice. The sound of them all singing together was so restful that in no time at all Jasmine was fast asleep.

Her mother quietly stopped singing, and tucked the covers around Jasmine's chin. She then put a little present on the pillow by Jasmine's head.

"Something for you to open when you wake up, Jasmine," she whispered.

"Now, come along you animals, time for us all to go to sleep."

The little bird in the tree stopped singing, and tucked its head under its wing. The goldfish started swimming a bit more slowly. The cat went back to its cushion under the window, and the dog stretched out lazily at the end of Jasmine's bed. Soon all of the animals had dozed off happily too.

In the morning, Jasmine woke up and had a good stretch.

Just then, she spotted the present Mum had left on her pillow.

"Ooh, a birthday present!" she cried, unwrapping it excitedly. Inside the bright wrapping paper was a little musical box. When Jasmine opened the lid, the box played the tune that her mother had sung to her the night before.

"Now I will always be able to get to sleep whenever I want to," said Jasmine happily and, from then on, she always could.